R up to the Ledge

Clare Bowes

illustrated by Scott Pearson

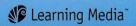

Learning Media™

Jason's teaching me to do ollies.

"Roll up to the ledge," Jason says.
I roll up to the ledge.

"Put one foot on the tail and
the other foot halfway
between the trucks."

I put one foot on the tail and
the other foot halfway
between the trucks.

"Slap the tail onto the ground.
Jump as it hits."

I'm on the ledge.
I slap the tail onto the ground.
I jump as it hits.

Crash!
I fall over.

"Try crouching
before you slap the tail," says Jason.

I try again.
I roll up to the ledge.
I put one foot on the tail and
the other foot halfway
between the trucks. I crouch.
I slap the tail onto the ground.
I jump.
I'm in the air with my feet
on the skateboard!

"Slide your front foot
over the front truck
and push!" shouts Jason.

Crash!
I didn't get over the ledge.

"You almost did it!" calls Jason.
"Watch this."

He rolls up, crouches, and
slaps the tail onto the ground.
He jumps and pushes his
front foot forward.
He's over! It looks so simple.

I try again.
I roll up, crouch,
slap the tail onto the ground,
and jump.
I'm in the air!
I push my front foot forward.
The skateboard and I go
over the ledge.

"You did it!" says Jason.
I feel good.
I do lots of ollies after that.

Then a kid from school
comes up to me.
"Can you show me
how to do ollies?" he asks.

"Sure," I smile.
"Roll up to the ledge," I say.
"Put one foot on the tail …"